How Bi-Yi-Yig is GOD?

BEV LAVIGNE

I0086884

How Bi-Yi-Yig is God?

Copyright © 2017 by Bev LaVigne

All rights reserved. No part of this book may be reproduced or transmitted in any form or by any means without written permission of the author.

ISBN 978-0-9991698-0-3

Published by:
Move Mountains Publishing, a GoBe'Do Enterprises LLC company.

How Bi-Yi-Yig is GOD?

Psalm 91

He that dwelleth in the secret place of the most High, shall abide under the shadow of the Almighty.

I will say of the Lord, He is my refuge and my fortress: my God; in him will I trust.

Surely he shall deliver thee from the snare of the fowler, and from the noisome pestilence.

He shall cover thee with his feathers, and under his wings shalt thou trust: his truth shall be thy shield and buckler.

Thou shalt not be afraid for the terror by night; nor for the arrow that flieth by day;

Nor for the pestilence that walketh in darkness; nor for the destruction that wasteth at noonday.

A thousand shall fall at thy side, and ten thousand at thy right hand; but it shall not come nigh thee. Only with thine eyes shalt thou behold and see the reward of the wicked.

Because thou hast made the Lord, which is my refuge, even the most High, thy habitation;

There shall no evil befall thee, neither shall any plague come nigh thy dwelling.

For he shall give his angels charge over thee, to keep thee in all thy ways.

They shall bear thee up in their hands, lest thou dash thy foot against a stone.

Thou shalt tread upon the lion and adder: the young lion and the dragon shalt thou trample under feet.

Because he hath set his love upon me, therefore will I deliver him: I will set him on high, because he hath known my name.

He shall call upon me, and I will answer him: I will be with him in trouble; I will deliver him, and honour him.

With long life will I satisfy him, and show him my salvation.

GOD

is bigger than the biggest tree.

GOD

is bigger than a manatee.

GOD

is not a miniature.

GOD

is big enough to be where you are...

...and lo, I am with you always, even unto the end of the world.
MATTHEW 28:20

GOD

is bigger than the thunder's roar!

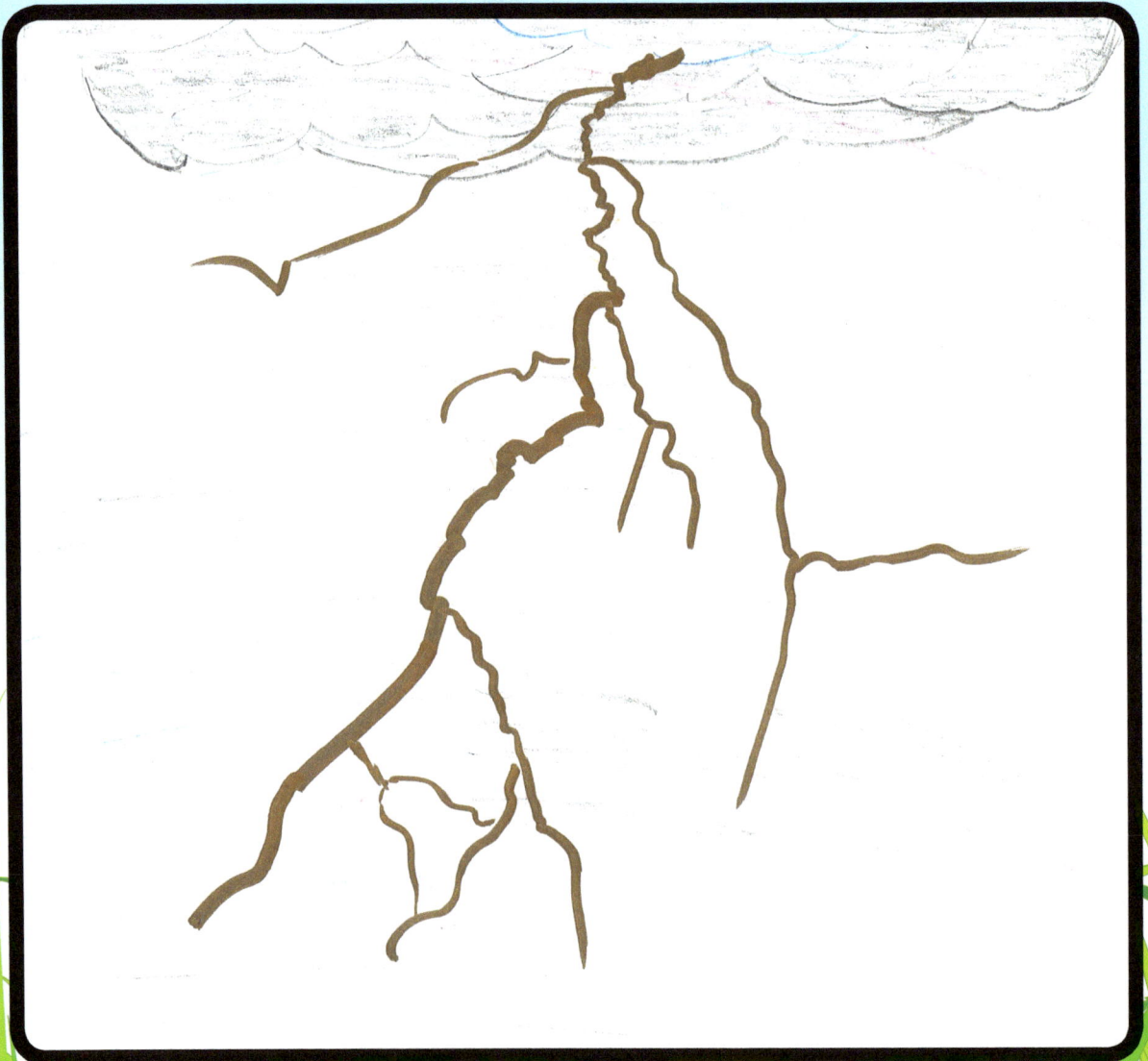

GOD

is bigger than every shore,
—even altogether.

 Baltic

 Black

 Caspian

Tyre

 Parana'

 Red

 Emirates

 Mediterranean

 North

 Japan

GOD

is bigger than all the world's big blue seas.

GOD

is big enough to hug you and me.

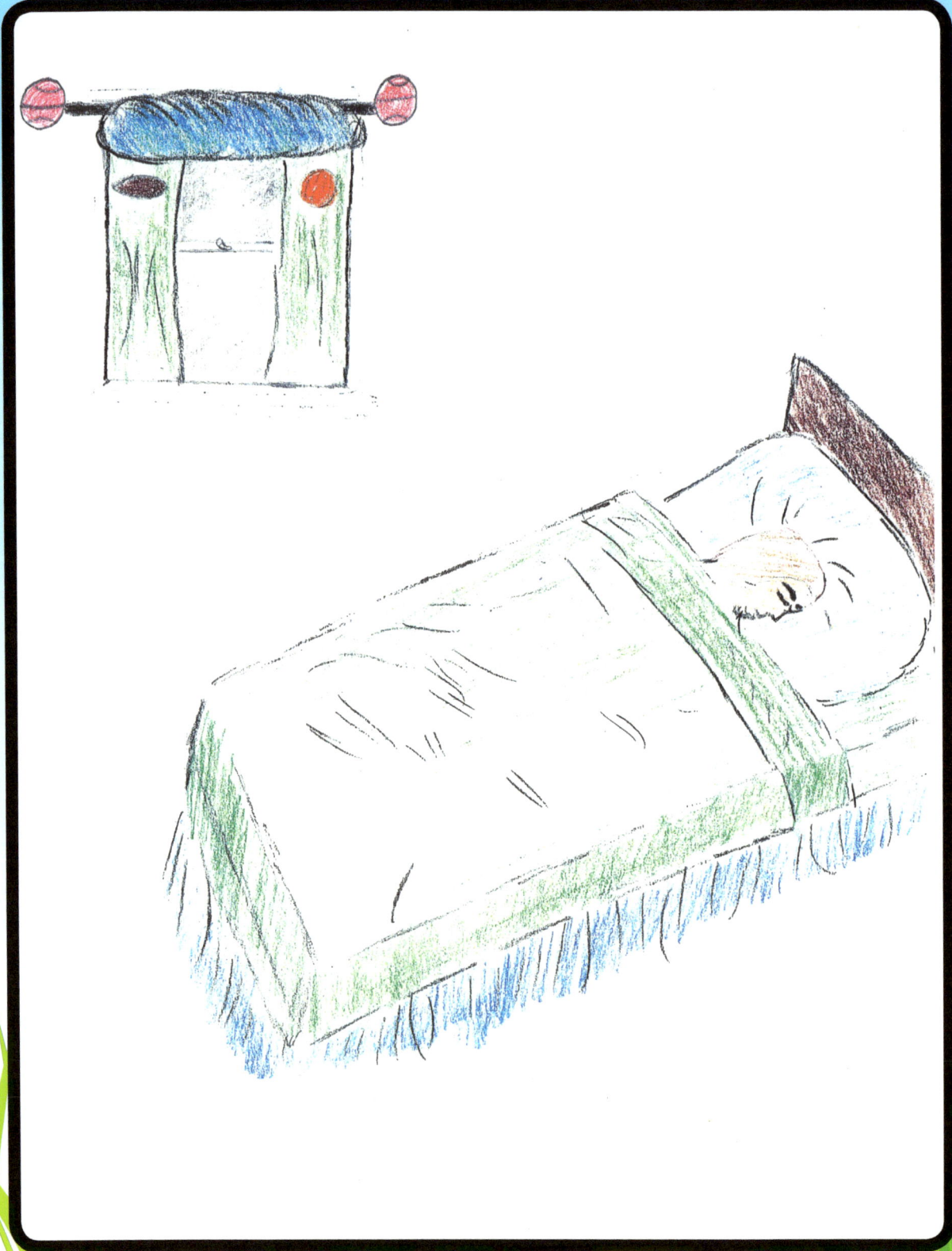

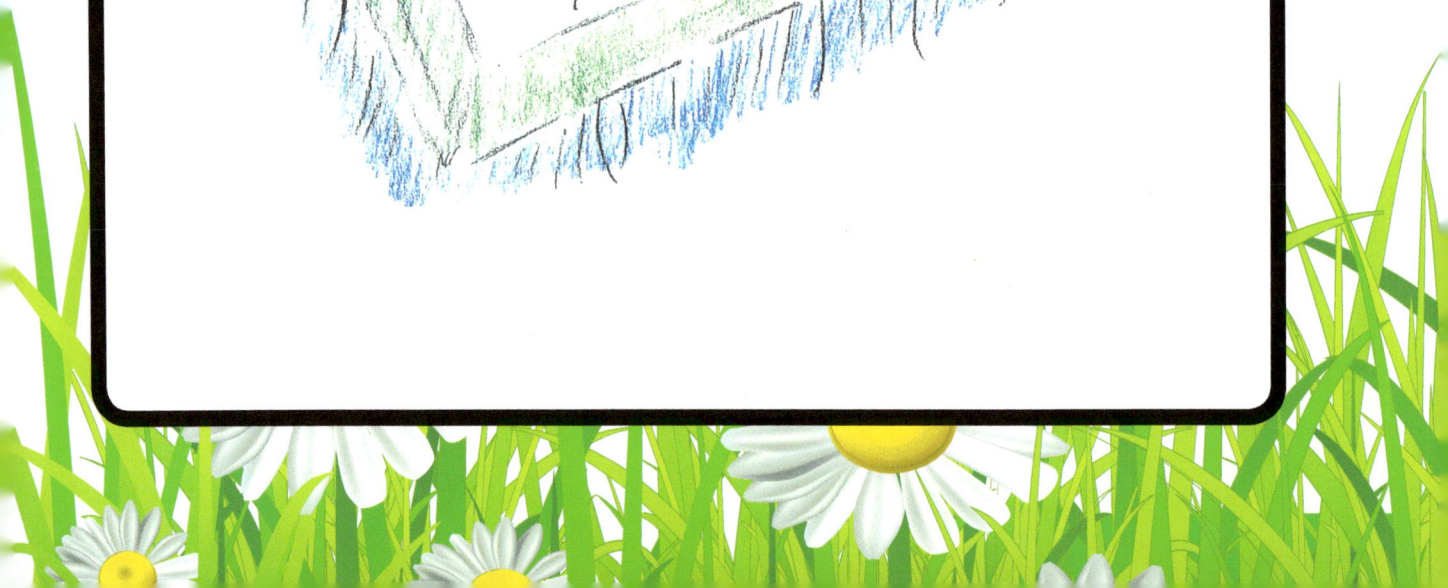

NO NEED

to be afraid of the dark at night.

> *...and the peace of God, which passeth all understanding, shall keep your minds through Christ Jesus.*
>
> PHILLIPIANS 4:7

GOD

is bigger than the brightest light!

And there shall be no night there; and they need no candle, neither light of the sun; for the Lord God giveth them light...

REVELATIONS 22:5

Oh, and about those witches,
goblins, werewolves and goons…

GOD

is so much bigger than them,
they seem like cartoons!

*And being found in fashion as a man he humbled himself,
and became obedient unto death, even the death of the cross.
Wherefore God also hath highly exalted him, and given him
a name which is above every name: That at the name of Jesus
every knee should bow, of things in heaven, and things in earth,
and under the earth that Jesus Christ is Lord to the Glory of
God the Father.*

PHILLIPIANS 2:8-10

GOD

is bigger than a Tyrannosaurus Rex.

Behold the fowls of the air: for they sow not, neither do they reap, nor gather into barns; yet your heavenly Father feedeth them. Are you not much better than they:

MATTHEW 6:26

But seek ye first the kingdom of God, and his righteousness; and all these things shall be added unto you.

MATTHEW 6:33

HE'S

even bigger than that big bully, Lex.

So that we may boldly say, The Lord is my helper, and I will not fear what man shall do unto me.

HEBREWS 13:6

Trust in the Lord with all thine heart; and lean not unto thine own understanding.

PROVERBS 3:5

Lord, please help me study in the best way for understanding.

$$E=mc^2$$

$$x = \frac{-b \pm \sqrt{b^2 - 4ac}}{2a}$$

A–Z?

$$y=mx+b$$

$$\begin{array}{r} 1,237,946,832 \\ \underline{\times\ 53,948} \end{array}$$

alliteration or onomatopoeia?

MOVE!!!

And Jesus said unto them,…If ye have faith as a grain of mustard seed, ye shall say unto this mountain, Remove hence to yonder place; and it shall remove; and nothing shall be impossible unto you.

MATTHEW 17:20

GOD

is bigger than the hardest homework, test or trial.

> *Happy is the man that findeth wisdom,*
> *and the man that getteth understanding*
>
> PROVERBS 3:13

WITH GOD,

through Jesus Christ in our hearts,
we can do all things!
With no denial!

Jesus saith unto him, I am the way, the truth, and the life: no man cometh unto the Father, but by me.

JOHN 14:6

I can do all things through Christ which strengtheneth me.

PHILLIPIANS 4:13

GOD

is bigger than that huge helping of spinach...

With His help, you could even finish,

before tomorrow's breakfast, or else…

To answer mom's first call,

Dishes!!!

OUCH!!!

or if off your bike you might fall.

GOD

is our Big Champion!

KING OF KINGS

α and Ω

LORD OF LORDS

He can help us through it all!

I am Alpha and Omega, the beginning and the end, the first and the last.

REVELATION 22:13

So, always remember our Big, Big,

GOD

He's bigger than the tallest tall.

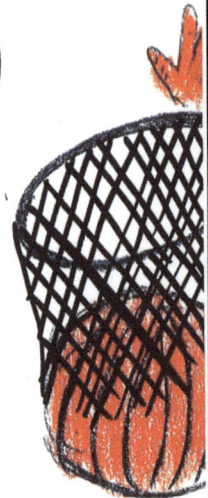

Bigger than the strongest strong.

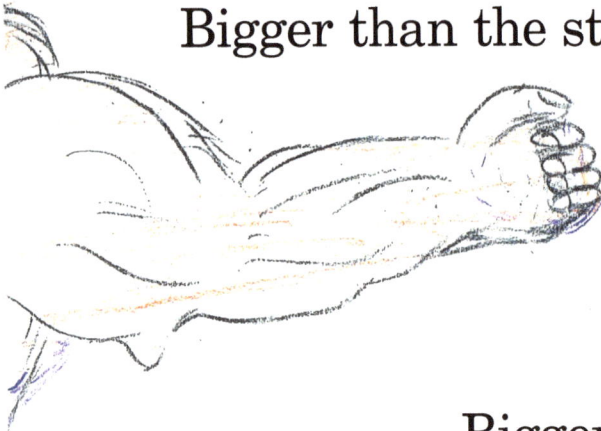

Bigger than the widest wide.

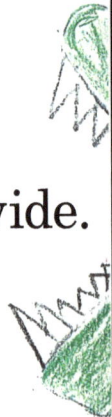

Bigger than the longest long.

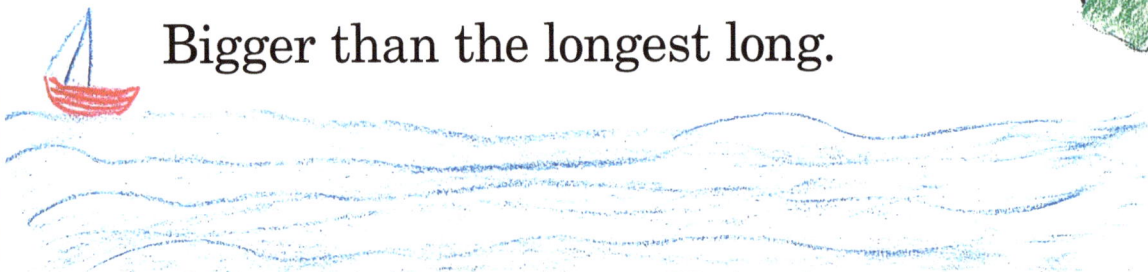

For He's bigger than it all!

Eeeek!

Even if it's from wall to wall.

For God hath not given us the spirit of fear; but of power, and of love, and of a sound mind.

2 TIMOTHY 1:7

Now, there is no mystery.

GOD

is bigger than anything we can see.

Now unto the King eternal, immortal, invisible, the only wise God, be honour and glory for ever and ever. Amen.
1 Timothy 1:17

*"Always remember
how Bi-yi-yig our God is."*
BEV LaVIGNE

www.ingramcontent.com/pod-product-compliance
Lightning Source LLC
Chambersburg PA
CBHW041236040426
42445CB00004B/43